NOTHING IS COMPLETE BEFORE IT IS BROKEN

Nothing is Complete Before it is Broken
new poems by Ole Wesenberg Nielsen

Some of the poems in this collection
were first published in Le Zaporogue
edited by Seb Doubinsky

First published in 2013 by
Leaky Boot Press
http://www.leakyboot.com

ISBN: 978-1-909849-02-0

NOTHING IS COMPLETE BEFORE IT IS BROKEN

new poems by

Ole Wesenberg Nielsen

LEAKY BOOT PRESS

CONTENTS

DODGE BALL

She doesn't want to get hit
I won't throw
Imagine if she caught the ball
So here we stand
And stare at each other
We both long for a final solution
The first one to speak loses

PRIVATEERING

Down at the harbor there is a street
Cranes are hanging and shadows standing
Ships are whispering and rust is creeping
The shiny railroad tracks end here
The ocean is far away, drowned maybe
I don't know

ROSE BUCKET

Fields of loathing words sounds like echoes
A past unvisited is a past never healed
I have paid the old fishwives at the harbor all I had
I wished for three wishes so that I will have no dreams

FREE VACANCY

There is a door to an empty room
it is open but no one enters
in that room you will find me

IF I HAD A TISSUE
WOULD I CRY?

Slowly some blood drips from your shores
you look like a gutted fish decaying in the fading light
I feel guilty like a fisher called Peter
maybe I was wrong to fuck you again
and sell your love for faded flowers on a well kept bed

SELF MAIDEN

The whispering sensation of your whiplash words
says more that any tango on marble floors
in this disco of thoughts and sequenced *clichés*
you make me realize something profound
There is no dick hard enough to penetrate you

GIRL IN A WHITE
MERCEDES

Still-life driving through summer rain
A pretty girl on the front seat
Blue eyes reflected in rear mirrors
The question is
Is she looking at you?
Every answer in your head
Will make a fool out of you

LOVE IN THESE MACHIAVELLIAN TIMES

On the balcony we shared a mental cigarette
Inhaled the fumes of regret
Agreeing to give up all shared dreams
Across the vast industrial harbor
The sun was rising too soon
Only for moments yet
We had this cold night in Venice

THE DEATH OF A
GARDEN GNOME

The flower thief
Has stolen the lawnmower
The rain drowns all noise
Or chance of pursuit
Like poetry without sound
We are all alone in this wet garden
Left for the crows to shit on

I USED TO BE A MAN,
NOW I AM A WORM

Sniffing the ground for the most secret feelings
There is no real emotion in the sky
Just clouds and they are fluffy and white
Even when it rains it is without any colors
The ground is full of all the small things in life
Even when you get stepped on from time to time
It's all worth it
At the bottom the soil is only richer

ARABIAN NIGHTS AND AMERICAN VIRGINS

Softly the shrapnel smashes though private Helen's lungs
In split seconds she falls to the desert ground
She can hear voices from somewhere all telling stories
In a dream not further than a bullet can fly

Šahrazad sits alone by a dried out waterhole
A young man stumbles towards her bleeding
There is a man called Ali and he is dying
He looks at Šahrazad in disgust—she is old
"Where are my virgins?" he cries in anger
Šahrazad takes a long look at Ali
"The 1001 nights have passed a long time ago"

JUST ANOTHER DAY AT WORK FOR A POET

Today is a loud day
I want to scream and shout
Let it all out whatever "it" is
I am on collision course with myself
Tearing anything apart just to be smart
Tonight is a drinking night
I bet that I will end up in a fight
Let it all get trashed or smashed
I am dancing naked with myself
And then being fucked by someone else

THE POWER OF ENDLESS DISCO

Dance motherfucker
Dance to the too friendly music
Lose yourself and party
Don't think about it
The tunes say you are happy
The voices tells you that you are having fun
Don't forget to buy this CD tomorrow

A DESERT HYMN

Deep in the desert lie some holy ashes
The wind can't blow them away
Rain can't rinse them from the sand
Once this was the bush that set the world on fire
Three tribes one God
Too many believers and threefold jealousy
One thing is written in the desert ashes:
Maybe none of them are insane.

WITH MY HEAD IN THE CLOUDS

There she stands
her smile is casually
directed the wrong way
hitting me where my heart should be
and here we go again
something starts to beat
it becomes a rhythm
and then a song
the kind you can't get out of your head
I will hum this crazy tune for weeks
not knowing what it means
before it makes or breaks me

HYMN TO THE LIPS OF
A PASSING WOMAN

Beware of the knives of Autumn leaves
as they fall into memories in the dirt.
Our summer has faded in the wind
the roads are wet with rain and slush
still the world is full of vibrant colors
one last hurray before life goes to sleep
becoming dreams of solstice wine
that tasted so good and smelled even better

FRANKENSTORM

This is one of these dark afternoons
Where the wind fights it self
like the end of a lovers quarrel
cold gusts hit the pavement
and shatters ashes from lost days

It is one of these fucking evenings
were memories resurface
from the depths of the sea
drowning everything in putrid water
ankle-deep in old shit again

Nighttime and the storm is coming
with icy rain, like a whip
tearing up my back making old scars bleed
from my viewpoint the sun seems so far away
I could burn myself thinking about it

THE SANTA CLAUS CLAUSE

Bowling for shadows
this river has changed
it is deeper than words
maybe true love exist
after all

FULL ACID RECON

We have singing pavement control
erase the writing on the wall
bad karma carrousel

HOW TO KILL A BUTTERFLY
WITH WORDS

There is a caterpillar staring at me
and I do not like it
it reminds me of what I could be
what a cheeky bastard
I bet it is up to something
concealing its true self
poetry hidden in plain sight

EVERY POEM IS A GYPSY

We have traveled far to go nowhere
a dead horse in a parking lot
slowly decomposing like unsaid words
in the stink of the surrounding culture
questions can roam anywhere
ask everything even the impossible
And travel where no poet has drunk before.

CASUAL SEMEN

I watch her ocean spread before me
Making my arousal more malicious

WINDSWEPT

a lonely old checkered scarf
is hanging on a roadside tree
it is windblown and wet
from the ever changing weather
someone lost it
someone found it
put it up for all the passers-by to see
nobody cares
everyone drives onwards
towards other hearts

THE MOON AND
THE MIDGET

When all thoughts crumble
and curling into a ball of pain
seems the best thing you can do
look the other way
into the rays of the orb of night
here in the darkest night it shines
and even insane joy is better
than a broken heart

POST PUSSY POSER

The chilling chat
by a daytime laundromat
freezes my sense of construction
and when she smiles at me
and the corners of this place
melt away into old ideas
and kisses long gone
I know now that I have
an apathy for deduction

DON'T-BELIEVE-IN-ANYTHING-FAKE HAIKU

This mind that
blows you away
is mine

PERFUMED MESS

(a Senryu poem)

Restless arms
Finite love
Silent pain

MINIMALIST MAGNOLIUM IN MY BRAIN

There is a perfect girl
living in the back of my mind
she does nothing
but hang around
I know she is not real
because she smiles

THE SACRAMENTS OF DEMOCRACY

Little voices
in the synagogue
sing of peace
No one listens
Everyone else is busy
slaughtering lambs

NAKED IS THE VAMPIRE

Suddenly a stake pierces my heart
As I fade into ashes again
I see her in the pure light of dawn
—Even from the grave I lust for her blood

FIRST STEPS

Thin soil binds us together
Every word is a flower or a fire
Weighed against unknown gales
We don't know if we are sowing
luscious seeds or salt

ALONE IN A PUDDLE OF PUKE

Laughter fills the fluffy seats
With ghost smiles
This place is a melting pot
Broken lights are dancing naked
Beer bottles slip on the too clean floor
my only escape lingers behind the bar

AUTUMN HAS A
WAY WITH WORDS

leaves are falling
through the thoughts
of lovers who once
were in love
with the trees

WHEN I STARE DOWN DOVES

The white paper tiger
says that its bite is the best
but when cowbells play
what is you nip worth then?
Maybe more than
your kisses could carry

SENRYU

Spring sunshine
A smile from rain clouds
Her wet hair

A SIREN SONG

Behold the death of the mermaid
—Her form cast ashore by cold waves
There is a taste, a faint scent of her
in all drinking water
decomposed,
but still bitter-sweet
none will know
that it is her broken heart

PINK IS NOT A POEM

Poets don't smile
Unless they have to
because poets know
that happiness
is a moment in life
that has no colour
unless you paint it
afterwards.

THE WICKED WHY

Meanwhile back in the jungle
Tarzan was getting naked
While Jane was running away
with a trucker called Dave
He soon
Found out that
she had gone
down the yellow brick road
looking for more than a jungle romance
and while Tarzan put on his underpants
he suddenly realized that
heroes almost never
get to keep the girl

A CROW KING'S FOLLY

All the dead clowns
smile without teeth or bite
as they watch yet another court jester
going to the scaffold
for telling the truth within a lie
—I hope he dies laughing
for all the world to hear

ROSES FOR AN AMERICAN FLOWER

(in memory of Rosa Parks)

Oh Rosa you sat down so hard
So that sparks
flew across the lanes
Divided a nation
You were the soul mother of kings
And stood up as tall
As a black statue of liberty

OLD SMELL

I have an old Stetson hat
it's smelling bad
like forgotten winds
It hangs in the garret
somewhere beyond my reach
Some days I tell myself
I will put that hat back on
and just ride away
Sometimes my wife tells me
to put away things in the attic
Life has become so full of things
filling out our living room
with responsibility
But that crown still waits
for something to happen
Nothing will
until my son grows up
and burns that goddamned cowboy hat

GOING FORWARD TO STAND STILL

There is a man walking by the road
the cars pass him by
the rain passes through him
he is heading along countless tracks
looking down as the landscapes changes
for him it does not matter
while he is travelling
his mind stands still
reliving that moment when life broke him
again and again
one foot in front of the other.

DRUNKARD EROTICS

Whiskey my old lover
I have smoked you
Inhaled your flower
tasted you bitterness
savoured the molten colours
yet still when I swallow
the memory of you
closes my eyes
and I smile
with the sensual pleasure
of the treasure you hide

AFFECTION FOR THE DEVIL

There is a time in between dream and nightmare
where you wonder if life would be different
then the pain of his fist sends you reeling
breaking you heart more than your jaw
soon he will beg for you for the mercy
that he does not have
forgiving him will not end the suffering
yet you do it again and again
until you get numb with it
in your addict you still crave for his devotion
any fix will do and all the suffering is forgotten
for a few moments of bliss in this hell hole
for me you are the ultimate conundrum
my question is simple
would you love someone
who does not hurt you?

THE CRYSTAL QUEEN

I hate the feeling of snow
its cold wet touch
when it settles on my face
it reminds me of cold hands
one snowflake seldom comes alone
they often build into a blizzard
that forms a landscape
filled with pure white
innocent has its beauty
that fades quickly
when it get mixed with dirt.

I AM NOT MORE THAN
A MINUTE AWAY

The mountains of the past stand tall
as the sun sets behind them
in a crescendo of red light
there is a silhouette in her eyes
even from afar
I can feel her.

HOW MANY TIMES CAN A CROW DIE?

There is a broken sparrow on the road
its hollow bones have snapped in the wind
better not to think about it
when there is a gale blowing
and you are swallowing the molten thoughts
that took you out in this misshapen weather
walking away only gives you some borrowed time
in the end you will have to finish what you started.

LOST IN MY OWN BOAT

Sometimes it is better to
cast off and see where you go
than sailing on unknown pavements
—in losing yourself in other seas
you might find something else.

THE DEATH OF A USED DRUGS SALESMAN

There is a conflict in my soul
maybe I should not do this any more
that is before the coffee kicks in
and words and sentences tumble out
it is like standing under a waterfall
cold and wet
yet so reviewing
that you feel on the top of the world
in the moments after you finished
then doubt sets in again
and you feel like a pusher
who just needs one more sale.

RETRO HEAVEN

Blank minds
empty choirs
singing loud
cold hymns
for no one

DRUGS ARE THE
BLIND MAN'S MUSIC

I have heard that some
people can hear colours
I can't even see more than
two sides of the same coin
I have tried
with alcohol or drugs
to get a similar effect
still I cant see nothing
I must be blind
still music takes me
to distant shores
like Homer on amphetamine
I use these travels
to write poetry about
what I have experienced
with these unseeing eyes.

SOME FISH ARE TOO BIG TO FRY

There are needles
in the waves
a conversation to
penetrate the skin
just below the waist
it feels like fucking a unicorn
something you wouldn't do
unless you really had to

THE DEAF EAR
OF DEMOCRACY

Freedom of speech
has no meaning
if you do not have
the right to be heard.

ORAL LESSONS

In the few guilty minutes
when you stare down at
the barrel in you mouth
before all sounds end
you have to decide
—did I deserve this
or am I fucked for nothing?

AS FERVENT AS BLACK BEER

Deep down in a cellar a man sits in the gloom
He is hitting his head against the endless wall
The piano isn't playing any more, so the music is his own
Along the foundation the creeps are crawling away
At the top of the cellar stairs where light starts
They are standing in line to hear a man
Playing in the gloom
They will applaud,
but not before they know he is so dead
He can't hit his head
Against the wall any longer

THE PLEASURE OF FALLING THROUGH THE FLOOR

I'm in that dim lit mystery room again
There is the cage with its silent rats
With their red eyes they stare back at me
If there is a door in this room they wouldn't know
These white rats don't know about restraint or choice
The light goes out again, this gloom smells funny
Find the walls I reason, then I'll find the door eventually
hours or what seems eons I have searched for the confines
Nowhere to go, I can't find the limits or they won't find me
Still there is an echo here that cast its form like a outline
a sound of feet moving upon sounds
of thousand feet standing still
Am I alone in this wasted room
or followed by others like me?

EARTH FARM

Headless chickens are running along
Outside my front door
From my window I can see
Them all dancing in a matching place
All listening to the same tune
Over and over and over
Until they can't hear anything
Not even the feet that trample them.

TO SMASH AN ELBOW THOUGH A RAINBOW

(dedicated to Kathrine O)

She is bound to cut herself
before she can feel colours again.

THE BULLY THEORY

You can get mugged
Beaten up or raped
And the police are never there
To help you out
but
If you protest too loudly
Look too different or is of another colour
The police are always there
To beat you up.

AND NOW TO SOMETHING ELSE

We interrupt this collection
for this important message!!
Democracy never happened
And now to commercials

MEDIA BLITZ

There is only one thing
in this Universe
that is faster
than the speed of light
And that is a politician
running away from responsibility

DAILY WISDOM

Beware of Socialists
with Gucci bags
one of them
is definitely
a fake

GHOST TOWN BLUES

I was born in
that one horse town
where the horse
fucking died.

SPRING FUNERAL

Cherry petals
on a newly washed car
death rides with us
every moment.

FROM THE MOUTHS OF DRUNKARDS

We will say everything
but reveal nothing.

THE ZEN IN SENRYU

Karma's joke is
that good things always happen
to very bad people

www.ingramcontent.com/pod-product-compliance
Lightning Source LLC
LaVergne TN
LVHW011412080426
835511LV00005B/501